EXIT
STRATEGIES

*The Perfect Excuse
for Any Social
Situation*

DAVID
JACOBSON

METRO BOOKS
New York

CONTENTS

PLAN A:

AVOIDANCE OR HOW TO SAY "NO"

PLAN B:

THE ART OF EXTRICATION OR HOW TO SAY "GOTTA GO NOW"

Introduction:
Avoidance or How to Say "No"

The great magician Harry Houdini could escape from handcuffs and straitjackets, even while hanging upside down locked inside a tank of water. That's all quite nice, but the real question is—could he escape a blind date from hell? Or from a boring business meeting? Or from having to view someone's vacation pictures?

In Plan A, you'll discover dozens of ways to dodge the venomous fangs of interpersonal obligation, from avoiding family gatherings to getting married. Some ploys are very situation-specific—the claim of a poorly fitting prosthetic leg makes an excellent excuse to avoid dancing, but a dodgy lip piercing that staples your mouth shut is more appropriate to begging off public speaking.

Throughout the book there are, however, some Universal Escapes. These specially marked passages include broadly useful and perennially popular ruses, such as "The Hospital Visit to an Elderly Relative Excuse," "An Attack of Food Poisoning," and "Sudden Temporary Onset of Blindness."

And though rarely employed, there's always "The Nuclear Excuse." This entails actually stating in brisk and succinct fashion why you really couldn't stand to babysit someone's creepy kids or attend another one of their grim get-togethers. Once you've dropped one of these pre-rehearsed devastating truth bombs, you'll want to exit the scene promptly!

It's all here. So be sure to take this book with you to parties, work, dates, or prison—any state of affairs you might want to get out of. This volume is the ultimate social insurance policy, the last word in life's loopholes, and the one thing you can't afford to avoid.

PLAN A:

Avoidance or
How to Say "No"

SMALL TALK ON MASS TRANSIT

YOU'RE TRAPPED ON A BUS, TRAIN, OR PLANE NEXT TO some unbelievably dull person who is inviting you to join them in their shop talk, description of physical ailments, and complaints du jour about the world, from pet political theories to incessant chatter about their work as a canned goods distributor or industrial catalog photographer. Here's what to do when a mellow trip threatens to become a slow-drip torture session:

The Assertive Donning of Earplugs Escape

Taking out a newspaper or a book only offers lily pads for the leapfrogging small-talker—"Never cared for that paper . . ."/"*Exit Strategies* sounds anti-social . . . ." Instead, the firm insertion of audio earbuds is the new default mode for: "It's been great, but I'm going to start ignoring you now."

The Endless Non-Existent Phone Call Escape

No audio headset? A cell phone is your next best friend. Pretend annoyance at the interruption of your new friend's fascinating commentary by a silent vibrating "ring." Then employ the following dialogue: "No, I didn't see it . . . It's how many pages?! . . . Oh for heaven's sake, you'd better read it to me." Roll your eyes and give an apologetic shrug to your silenced seatmate. You're now free to do whatever you'd like, occasionally mumbling into your phone, "No, read me that too; the devil's in the fine print."

The Difficulty Hearing Escape*

Up to 3 million people worldwide have narcolepsy, which can cause sufferers to suddenly drop off into dreamland for a few seconds or up to several minutes at a time.* After explaining the situation up front, nod off whenever your yakking neighbor says more than three consecutive sentences. Jolt awake, mutter apologies, and ask them if they wouldn't mind repeating what they just said. Continue until they're exasperated into silence.

* Depending on your religious beliefs, faking an ailment like this could ultimately send you to a place where you'll be seated with the small-talker for all eternity. But perhaps you can make a charitable donation down the road to smooth things over.

Other Nightmare Venues

→ An elevator: If someone interrupts your daydreams, back them off with wearisome quasi-profundities: Point out that even the contextualized experience of vertical transportation renders no objectively valid meaning.

→ Public toilets: If someone tries chatting from the sink or adjacent stall, take a bill from your wallet, extend it under the divider and say: "There's no toilet paper in here, would you have change for a five?" This should yield an appropriately horrified silence.

ATTENDING A
FRIEND'S PLAY

YOUR ARTSY FRIEND IS GREAT—EXCEPT FOR THE ARTSY part: *Waiting for Godot* staged at freezing bus stops/a gallery full of huge white canvases with tiny stick figures titled Untitled #417-433a/coffeehouse rants delivered squeaky-voiced from inhaled helium to protest modernity's "castration of the spirit." Here's how to artfully evade their next invite:

→ By coincidence, your own play, opening, dance, or reading is at the same date and time. Call this "synchronicity"—it sounds artier.

→ As a wry commentary on the preponderance of the bourgeois and the philistine in contemporary society, you're avoiding all art galleries, dance, and live performances in favor of snacking in a recliner and watching infomercials. You're hoping to get a grant so you can relocate to a museum and display your nihilistic anti-aesthetic 24/7.

→ You can't wait to attend their performance! And wouldn't it be cool if you repeated all their lines right after they said them, making a crazy echo effect in the back of the theater?

→ Decline by haiku:

> *"I won't be at your/show, because your 'art' baffles/and leaves me queasy."*

→ Perform a dance: Helpless amid their kitschy crap (fetal position) you break free (fists in all directions) and lunge (lunge) to freedom (cartwheels)!

→ Use a failsafe medical excuse:

A) You've got a repetitive stress injury of the wrists and must avoid bravura art that evokes your rapturous applause.

B) You've got a slipped disk in your neck and must avoid powerful performances that make you recoil from their bitter truths.

UNIVERSAL ESCAPE #1:

The Hospital Visit to an Elderly Relative

In the poker game of invites and turn-downs, no card trumps this one. Just say your favorite great-uncle has fallen ill. The beauty of this imaginary aged relative is that little detail is required ("Apparently it's his spleen this time . . .") and they can be used repeatedly.

FAMILY GATHERINGS

IT'S A HOLIDAY DINNER, SUNDAY BRUNCH, OR A FULL-
blown reunion. Once again it's time to face your relatives: bitter
Uncle Ralph with his nasty political views; the dim cousins who
keep trying to fix you up, even though you're engaged; the sibling-
in-law rivals insisting that your income's a pittance or that you've
sold out. Here's how to notify your next of kin you're going AWOL:

The Volunteering Excuse

You can't come because you're helping those without wonderful families.
You're ladling gravy in a soup kitchen, answering a crisis hotline, or visiting
elderly shut-ins. You not only get a free pass, you put Uncle Ralph in his
place and one-up your rivals.

The Scalding Memoir Excuse

You can't make it because your new memoir about your horrible family full
of hateful uncles, dull cousins, and insecure siblings-in-law is arriving in
bookstores. You're tied up doing media interviews and talk shows. You'll
send them all signed copies of *Family Reunions with Satan's Minions*.

The Entering Rehab Escape

If excuses fail and you're trapped again, start drinking heavily. Then, call
several friends from the bathroom. They can show up and, with apologies
to your relatives, perform an "intervention," confronting you about your
"problem." Later, at the bar, it's a full night of drinks on you.

BECOMING
A GODPARENT

TWO CLOSE FRIENDS HAVE ASKED YOU TO BE THE GOD-parent of their baby. This is no time to wax sentimental and buy a "World's Best Godparent" mousepad. Accede to this and you're signing up for decades of birthday parties, graduation ceremonies, and babysitting "opportunities." Act now!

→ You're honored, but wouldn't their much more successful friend be a much better choice? Someday they could help the kid out with their important connections.

→ You're deeply moved, but wouldn't it be better to bestow this honor on their ne'er-do-well friend in honor of him/her being six weeks/days/hours sober? Showing your faith in him/her could be just the thing to help them turn their life around.

→ You can't be godparent since you're a strict existential atheist; but you'd be glad to show up in the child's life, like the hand of fate in a random and indifferent universe, to either dispense candy or rap their noggin with a mallet.

PUBLIC SPEAKING

FOR MANY, THE FEAR OF PUBLIC SPEAKING (TECHNICAL name: glosso-phobia) is a terrifying ordeal worse even than the fear of bald mothers-in-law who are also clowns (technical name: pelado-pentheracoulro-phobia). But there are plenty of rational reasons to dodge speech-making: the risk of a work presentation gone horribly awry, drawing a blank during a eulogy, or blurting out something inappropriate while trying to ad lib a wedding toast. The right excuses, spoken privately, might avoid public shame:

The Video Presentation Excuse

Thanks to camcorders and webcams, the most speech-o-phobic can give their talk to a non-judgmental audience of none, then just hit play for the crowds. Just make sure there's nothing private on that recording.

The Short and Sweet Excuse

If brevity is the soul of wit, it's also the thing that can get you out of most public speaking. Just make quick work of handing off speaking duties. This may come as a complete surprise to the person you're suddenly introducing, but if they wind up hemming and hawing then they are the ones who screwed up, after your elegantly pithy introduction: "Thanks for coming, now I'd like to introduce someone whose reputation speaks for itself, my personal hero in this industry . . . "

The Lost Voice Excuse

It only takes pointing at your throat, then clutching it to express pain—which any chimp can do. You simply can't go on. Add cherry-flavored lozenges to impart a scary redness to the back of your throat.

The Temporary Insanity Excuse

You simply can't give the speech because the only way you can overcome your stage fright is to picture the entire audience naked. And once you do that you become visibly aroused—very visibly. So you have to think of something non-arousing and by then you've completely lost track of what you're trying to say.

The "How Does This Sound So Far?" Non-Excuse Excuse

Approach whomever requested that you speak and ask to run a few lines of your talk by them:

> **EULOGY** *"... and so they abruptly left the mother/father of their kids for the very person who'd wind up cheating on them with their former spouse! But really, those were the good times..."*

> **WEDDING TOAST** *"Soon after they met, the bride and groom both confided in me that the other person seemed like 'a very short-term thing.' In fact, they represented a 'romantic compromise' they'd only make if they had no other options..."*

> **RETIREMENT DINNER SPEECH** *"So he said, 'We'll just lift figures from the inventory column each quarter and put them into booked sales, take our performance bonuses to the bank, and by the time the big boys are any wiser, we'll be retired...'"*

> **CONFERENCE KEYNOTE ADDRESS** *"To those who call our industry dull, wasteful, sloppy, incestuous, and corrupt to the core, I say you may indeed have a valid point..."*

MEETINGS AT WORK

MOST WORKPLACE MEETINGS SEEM DESIGNED TO WASTE your time, sap your spirit, or tell you what you already know. Do your employer—and yourself—a favor by leaving them to the agenda-shuffling company deadwood. Here's how:

The Out-of-the-Office Escape

You're sorry but you have to be across town for a big meeting—potential new client, very hush-hush, hopefully you'll have good news for everyone next week/month/year. Thanks to laptops and cell phones you could just lay low in a café across town, but it's best to go home and nap so as not to be spotted.

The Here-but-Not-Here Escape

The wonders of Skype, emails and phone calls allow you to fill a seat at a big staff meeting while still getting your day's work done—typing and talking into your ear-piece phone. You can always pretend that you're avidly taking notes on the proceedings (for example, Announcement of Bring Your Trained Bird of Prey To Work Day—what could possibly go wrong?) and/or creating a play-by-play podcast of the meeting for those traveling or based in the company's new Mumbai, Dubai, and Antarctica branch offices.

The Outsourced Performance Review Escape

You've briefed lower-cost employees in that new Mumbai branch office and arranged for them to hold the meeting instead (that is, discussing your job performance and raise). Given the time difference, they'll be done tomorrow morning. As soon as you get their lower-cost meeting's minutes via e-mail you'll forward them to all concerned.

The Incited Riot Escape

Generate a rowdy hubbub that will let you slip out. Your possible suggestions include:

A) Replace the sexual harassment policy with training in Aikijujutsu, a Japanese samurai martial art—that way inappropriate behavior is dealt with forcefully and on the spot.

B) Require the board to undergo drug testing before they approve top executives' pay.

C) Build company morale by using competitors' products as speed bumps in the employee parking lot.

The Fake Food Poisoning Excuse

The most sublime of escapes is the fake food poisoning excuse. After all, it's a sudden onset, swift recovery, could-happen-to-anybody-anytime-anywhere sort of thing. Whether warding off unwanted advances at the bar ("Before you try kissing me, there's something you should know . . .") or escaping the office holiday party ("Could've been salmonella in my eggnog . . ."), it's the ejector seat par excellence. No need for a back story, no one will seek details of your intestinal pseudo-suffering.

So if you're trapped in a new logo brainstorm session, it's time to grab your belly with visible distress and head for the door. Either take your laptop to an executive restroom or enjoy a lazy afternoon in the park. Return later, stalwart and stoic: "Feeling . . . better . . . what did I miss?"

EXPENSIVE
RESTAURANT MEALS

THEY'RE THE YOUNGEST PERSON TO MAKE PARTNER AT Bigg, Staxx, & Kasch. And you? You're in "the helping professions" or "an excuse-book writer." Now they've asked you to dinner at El Caviarrio, where picking up the check could give you a financial hernia. How do you handle it?

→ Decline their invitation by honestly explaining you're on a tight budget— no need to cite daydreams about selling a kidney to pay off student loans. If they insist on covering your meal, offer to tackle the tip—after all, you won't be going back there.

→ You're friends, right? Remind them of life back on Earth. Explain that you may be late because your favorite pawn shop gets busy near mealtimes. Then suggest a nice but more reasonable place around the corner.

→ Call from your car parked at a cheap take-out place two blocks away. Shout over your own honking horn about an impossible traffic jam. You'll make it there in time for dessert—then take them out for a beer at a pub for normal people.

DANCING

THERE ARE LOTS OF TIMES YOU'D ENJOY DANCING; FOR example while home alone, wearing headphones, and in your underwear, but not now: the music's painfully uncool, there's no one else on the dance floor, and/or the person approaching you has the frothing enthusiasm of a lunatic exhibitionist. Without being anti-social, here are your anti-dancing steps:

→ You'd love to, but you're recovering from a badly sprained ankle or a rupture of the anterior cruciate knee ligament (practice saying anterior cruciate so it rolls off the tongue).

→ Of course you like to dance, but you've just never been able to get the hang of the Argentine Tango/Macarena/Hokey Pokey.

→ Sorry, but you promised (look around expectantly) you'd save the night's first dance for [name of your favorite Disney animation character plus a brand of beer]. Perhaps later . . .

→ Your latest fake leg doesn't fit very well. Sometimes it slips clean off, causing you to fall and hit your head—again.

→ You'd love to dance, just not to this song. It was playing in the background when you lost your virginity, so it would feel too weird. (Bonus points if the song is "The Hokey Pokey," "YMCA," or "I'm Too Sexy.")

→ You'd love to dance, just not to this song. (This works best if you haven't already used the above excuse, but may be a back up if the same person approaches you again.) It was playing in the background when your best childhood friend was killed in a tragic [choose only one] skeet shooting/ body-piercing/mechanical bull-riding accident. "I'd feel like I was dancing on his/her grave."

→ Even the most attractive people are less approachable when they are dripping with perspiration . . . Before going out, pursue a vigorous aerobic workout. Try 20 brisk minutes on a stationary bicycle or visit a steam sauna fully clothed. This should leave you too slimy and reeking for even the person most desperately seeking a dance partner.

→ Normally, you'd love to but you're getting over an inner ear infection that causes nauseating vertigo and a tendency to fall over and hit your head.

→ You've been told such vigorous motions could dislodge the blood clot in your leg, sending it to a lung. For best delivery, start to rise, muttering, "Oh, to hell with doctors." Then slump back, grasping your side: "Probably . . . just . . . a stitch!"

EXCUSES FOR HIM

Confide your lack of underwear (it's a long story), so you'd run a high risk of injury.

You've already had a few too many, and you're afraid that if you move too much, the room may start to spin and then who knows what will come up.

The vigorous motion may cause your recent hernia incision to reopen.

EXCUSES FOR HER

Confide in a teeth-gritted whisper: "I'd love to, but I have the worst PMS/pre-PMS/post-pre-PMS."

You're waiting for a faster- or slower-paced number. Always insist the rhythm is not quite right for you to take to the floor. You can always add: "more syncopated" or "more samba-esque" to further muddy the waters.

Offer to go for a walk instead. Guys are suckers for this and really, you only have to walk him as far as the nearest bar or beer cooler. At least you won't have to dance with that loser.

DINNER PARTY INVITATIONS

SURE, DINNER PARTIES OFFER THE APPEAL OF A fabulous meal, fine wine, and convivial friends. But you've learned whose invites to avoid—the meal will be an experimental disaster, the wine an expectorant cough syrup, and the conversation inane. For those, we've cooked up your excuses:

The Self-Sacrifice for an Allergic Friend Excuse

It's your new boyfriend/girlfriend/spouse/child. They're severely allergic to nuts, seeds, shellfish, wheat, dairy, soy, corn, candy corn, yellow food dyes numbers 5 and 6, and the vowels e, i, and u in alphabet soup. Even if they abstained, if you ate some of those foods and then kissed them, they could still break out in deadly hives.

The Serious Eater Non-Excuse Excuse

You'd love to come, especially now that you're in training as a competitive eater. Technically, a gurgitator. You've been stretching out your stomach by guzzling jugs of water and holding your esophagus open so you can stuff down meats or pies faster without gagging. Ask what lubricants—you mean condiments—they'll be serving!

The Dreadful Babysitter Excuse

Last time you went to a dinner party, you came home and caught the babysitter on the couch in a flagrant embrace with their squeeze. You crept back out and waited, but you fell asleep and only woke at 2 a.m. Then they demanded overtime. You got in an argument and now they won't sit for you anymore.

THE NUCLEAR EXCUSE

Remember, delivering The Big N.O. is like yanking a bandage off a hairy body part: You've got to work fast. Practice blurting out the following in a single breath:

"I can't make it to your dinner party because the average life expectancy even in the most advanced nations is about 80 years, which breaks down to 700,800 hours, and I'll spend a third of that asleep (subtract 233,600); and 40 hours a week for 40 years at work (subtract 76,800); then there's commuting and being stuck in traffic jams (subtract 23,400); watching bad TV shows and re-runs I didn't like the first time (19,200); plus bathroom time, flossing, and volunteer work (17,841). That only leaves 329,959 hours of life to really enjoy—so you can see I don't have two or three of those to waste on tasteless cuisine, cheap zinfandel, and a gathering of negative-I.Q. mouth breathers."

GIVING ADVICE

YOUR FRIEND, NEIGHBOR, AND/OR EX-CELLMATE WANTS to know if they should: a) quit their unfulfilling job; b) leave their not-so-great lover; or c) sell their lame stocks to buy that alluring condo. You could tell them what they want to hear, but then you'll feel responsible if it all goes hideously wrong. Here's how to avoid giving advice:

→ You're just too close to them to see the situation objectively. Add that you support them 100 percent in whatever they ultimately decide to do!

→ Should they dump their stock portfolio to buy an unseen pasture on the remote Mongolian outback that should appreciate as the world's appetite for yak milk grows? Pretend to think about it, arching one brow and tapping your fingertips together, then ask intensely: "What do you think you should do?" Repeat until they're sick of talking about it.

→ They say: "But didn't you also quit your steady job selling fancy dress shoes and leave your longtime love for a prison escapee you'd only met on the internet?" You say: "No, my situation was very different; I sold casual dress shoes."

→ Learn to say, as if it is just occurring to you, the lines of the German poet Rainer Maria Rilke:

> *"Have patience with everything unresolved in your heart and try to love the questions themselves as if they were locked rooms or books written in a very foreign language. Don't search for the answers, which could not be given to you now, because you would not be able to live them. And the point is, to live everything. Live the questions now. Perhaps then, someday far in the future, you will gradually, without even noticing it, live your way into the answer."* Then add: *"Look at the time, my favorite reality TV show is on!"*

→ Just get it over with by repeating uselessly generic one-liners:

> *"Whatever you do, follow your heart."* Freely add, *"or your pancreas."*

> *"You'll always regret the things you don't do."* If asked for clarification, add *"plus about 57 percent of the things that you do."*

> *"Whatever you ultimately decide, don't second-guess yourself."* If asked for clarification, add *"unless it's a total disaster."*

HELPING SOMEONE MOVE

IT SOUNDS MEAN-SPIRITED, BUT THIS IS A CLASSIC CASE of no good deed going unpunished. You'll be the only one to show up, then suffer through endless hours of disorganized schlepping. After spending your entire day off helping out, you'll be muscle-sore, dirty, and depressed. Just don't do it:

The Injury That Prevents Lifting Excuse

Fake an injury that prevents lifting. It can be a slipped spinal disc, a healing hernia, or even a repetitive stress injury (damn these computer keyboards!). A "pulled muscle" makes an obvious yet irrefutable last-minute excuse.

The Moral Reservations Excuse

You don't feel right taking a job away from a "professional mover." Do we really want to live in a society where guys strong enough to carry couches, mahogany armoires, and pianos up and down stairs are out of work and roaming the streets?

The Condition of Your Parole Excuse

Sorry you can't help. You see, as a teen you pulled a practical joke. You emptied out a friend's house while they were away and hid all their stuff in a big barn! But that barn turned out to be the site of an estate auction. Anyway, you can't go near moving trucks for years to come, as a condition of your parole.

The Condition of Your Parole Excuse II

The last person you helped move . . . It's a long story and the lawsuit is still pending. There was a lot of breakage and it turned out it wasn't really their stuff that you were moving. Anyway, it's best if you don't "help" with any other "moving" for now.

UNIVERSAL ESCAPE #2:

The Temporary Paralysis Excuse

It sounds extreme, but heavy guilt-tripping requires an equally heavy counterbalance. You need something like Guillain-Barré syndrome, a typically non-fatal disorder causing paralysis that many victims recover from in a few months. If even that's too sick, morbid, and not likely to slip by a co-worker or neighbor who sees you every day, there's always Hysterical Paralysis (strictly emotional in onset and duration), which will get you out of not just moving, but giving people rides across town in your new car, too.

PLEASE NOTE: In these situations you do not want to claim strokes, A.L.S., or serious spine injuries. Not only are these terrible tragedies afflicting millions that you should never mock, but they're too complex to fake.

BEING REACHED

YOUR BOSS NEEDS YOU TO COME IN FOR OVERTIME. YOUR mom/lawyer/client wants to chat when you've got a romantic evening or sleep-in morning planned. Cell phones, e-mail, instant messaging, and overnight delivery make it ever harder to simply be out of touch. How can you make sure the bell tolls not-right-now for thee?

The Semi-Truth Excuse

You got their message a week ago but you were busy and this is the very first chance you've had to get back to them. Remember, the quicker you respond the more people expect it, thus causing a vicious downward spiral of availability.

The Spam Filter Excuse

You never got their e-mail because of your hyperactive spam filter. You're terribly chagrined, and don't know why it would have screened out their e-mail in particular. Confide that they wouldn't believe the misspelled come-ons that do get through.

The Auto-Reply Excuse

Once you receive an e-mail from someone or about something you're avoiding, create a fake auto-reply: "I'll be overseas and unreachable until [whatever date sets you free] working with Habitat for Humanity to build thatched dung yurts in Gadzookistan."

The Big Oops Response Excuse

Send a generic reply you'd usually send to your mom—"Sorry to have been out of touch, just working extra long and hard"—to your boss, and vice versa: "I'd like to cut back my hours so I can spend more time visiting my parents." When they catch up with you a day or two later, insist: "But I got right back to you!"

The Epic Eclipses Excuse

You had your ringer off because you attended the complete *Lord of the Rings* trilogy (10 hours), went straight to an intermission-free *Hamlet* (four hours), then stopped to visit your ailing great-uncle (no ringers on the ward!).

The Computer Virus Excuse

It's the old "I'm too sick to come in to work and if I did I'd give everyone else this awful bug I've got" excuse for the cyber age. You needed to get your PC/cell phone/Blackberry virus-free before you could respond. It's a viral worm spread through instant messaging, but it can even infect cellular phone calls, sending porn to everyone on the recipient's contacts list.

The Bad Water/Electronics Timing Excuse

You didn't get their message because your cell phone, Blackberry, etc. was utterly ruined after:

A) a taxi drove through a puddle from a broken water main;

B) you dove into a river to save a child; and/or

C) you tried that crazy log flume ride!

VIEWING HOLIDAY
PHOTOGRAPHS

IT MAY BE THEIR ENCYCLOPEDIC WEDDING/HONEYMOON
album, a camera phone full of snapshots from their vacation, or a
website devoted to their darling new addition. As Bogart meant to
say, here's not looking at you—or your kids:

The Missing Glasses Excuse

You're so absent-minded! You've left your reading glasses at home and
without them everything would just be a blur—and you simply wouldn't be
able to do the photos justice. What's that? No, really, no need to describe
each photo—you'll do your best to remember your glasses the next time
you see them and check out the pics yourself. To make this excuse more
believable, try bumping into the odd person as you weave your way off
down the street.

The Delayed Viewing Escape

It has been scientifically proven that for each additional 48 hours you can
postpone viewing other people's devastatingly dull photos/videos, you are
10 percent less likely to ever have to sit through them. So say you don't
have the time right now. Pick a future date to enjoy them at your leisure,
say two weeks from now. And when that date arrives, postpone again.
Repeat as necessary until said owner of pics gets the hint.

The Generic Commentary Escape

If they leave their photo album with you and/or e-mail you a link to an online gallery, you can still skip viewing them if you have a pleasant comment or two to offer or e-mail back. Here's how to respond without actually looking:

WEDDINGS: *It looks like it was a beautiful day—I'm sorry I missed it.*

BIRTHDAY: *It was great to see you among all your friends. What a shame I had to work that night.*

VACATION: *I feel like I'm seeing that place with a fresh pair of eyes! The view from where you were staying was really special.*

BABY: *Aw . . . they look just like your merged DNA, don't they?*

PET: *I've never seen such a lively, yet perfectly restful [type of animal].*

NEW HOUSE: *That front door looks so knockable! And those windows must let in photons of light! It's like a page from a real estate brochure!*

LIVING TOGETHER

YOU'VE ALREADY GOT A TOOTHBRUSH AND UNDERWEAR at each other's places. And it does seem wasteful to pay two rents. Your squeeze thinks it's time for "the next level of intimacy," but you thought that meant sharing a fondue fork. When you're not ready to merge addresses, try these excuses instead:

The Moving Too Fast Excuse

You haven't dated through the ups and downs of an entire presidential term. They don't even know your secret nickname for your second smallest toe. (Note: This may be less effective if you are residents in an old age home.)

The Romantic Ruination Excuse

How will you keep the sexy spark alive when you're routinely prying each other's hair from drains and overhearing gargling—or worse? And that's not even mentioning the fatal discovery that your darling is a compulsive wee-hours consumer of doggie biscuits.

The Cleanliness Issues Excuse

You consider your beloved a "neat freak" because they always have to "see what's underfoot," don't believe that a fork with old food hardened between the tines has "evolved" into a spork, or that what's under your couch is "a really cool dust bunny hutch."

The Interior Decorating Trust Issue

You've overheard them talking in their sleep and it sounds like they want to repaint your entire place in their favorite team's loud colors and/or put up girly lace curtains and a floral stencil wall trim. With that threat hanging over you, you don't feel your relationship would survive moving in with one another.

The Just No Space Excuse

There isn't room for them to move in (or vice versa), as you maintain a complete archive of all of your junior sports trophies, school quizzes, work memos, stuffed pets, and other memorabilia that you just can't bring yourself to throw away. You've got to think about that big museum they'll build after you're a famous historical figure.

The Family Disapproval Excuse

If word of your shacking up got back to your very traditional maternal grandmother, she'd disown you. And you're sure she's got a tidy sum tucked away somewhere—surely your beloved wouldn't want you to miss out on your inheritance by moving in together now rather than in, say, five years' time?

GETTING MARRIED

YOU'VE BEEN GOING OUT FOR—IS IT TUESDAY?—TWO years, seven months, and three days. Now the "M" word crops up regularly. Your beloved is gung-ho and you, well . . . you have trouble committing to an extended cell phone plan. Before being joined in the legal epoxy of holy matrimony, you'd like to mull and procrastinate for another millennium. Here are some rules of disengagement:

The Extra-Special Proposal Excuse

You're waiting until the moment is just right: There's currently a seven-month waiting period to have your proposal posted on the stadium scoreboard during your team's next really significant league match.

The Pre-Nuptial Agreement Excuse

True, your assets amount to a Troll Dolls of the World keychain set, a Complete Women/Men of Tahiti drink coaster set, and the dog-stained hand-me-down couch—but it all needs to be appraised. Then the appraisal has to be notarized, the pre-nuptial agreement drawn up, and then . . .

The We Haven't Reached True Emotional Intimacy Excuse

You can't bring yourselves to share your ATM PINs or e-mail account passwords—and that's really bugging you. Sometimes you'll start to say it, but only ******* comes out. How can you be wed while harboring such crucial secrets?

The Child-Raising Differences Excuse

A) You'd want to allocate child-rearing responsibilities precisely as they were depicted in that documentary about penguins.

B) No baby carriages for your kids: They walk, crawl, or stay home.

C) As for religion, you'd want them raised as strict Rotisserians. That'll mean worshipping meat in shop windows as it turns slowly on a spit.

The We're Just Too Young Excuse

"Our enthusiasms are still evolving. If we agreed to a lifelong union now we'd regret it if one of us decides to become a priest/nun, a non-ironic ABBA fan, addicted to breath mints or a nudist."

The Conflicting Career Goals Excuse

"Right now we're both dog groomers. But what if one us becomes the ruthless kingpin of a underworld crime syndicate and the other a hard-boiled cop dedicated to bringing down the mob at any cost? Our marriage would be an absolute hell."

NUCLEAR EXCUSES FOR HIM

"Sorry, but I could never marry a woman who still stacks her bed with plush toys, each with its own special personality; nor someone who says if I was being burned at the stake during the Dark Ages she wouldn't necessarily speak up and get in trouble herself but she would only pretend to help look for kindling; I realize saying this now instead of a simple 'I Do' in front of 150 people who have traveled from three continents is perhaps not the best timing on my part but there you have it."

NUCLEAR EXCUSES FOR HER

"Sorry, but I could never marry a man who refers to his penis as The Little Engine that Could or Thomas the Tank Engine or simply Frodo Baggins; nor someone who when you ask if you look fat in a particular pair of jeans responds, 'Compared to what other land and sea mammals?'; I realize saying this now instead of a simple 'I Do' in front of 150 people who have traveled from three continents is perhaps not the best timing on my part but there you have it."

BACHELOR/BACHELORETTE PARTIES AND OVERSEAS WEDDINGS

YOU'RE GENERALLY UP FOR A GOOD NIGHT OUT WITH your friends but more often than not want to dodge the general debauchery and sobering bar tab that comes with a bachelor/bachelorette party. You're supposed to be in their wedding party on a distant resort island and buy a gift from a registry list that would've suited Marie Antoinette with a plutonium Amex card. To retain their friendship and your solvency, you need a lacy veil of excuses:

The Stripper Excuse

You've just realized that the stripper at the bachelor/bachelorette party is your ex. You'd better make yourself scarce before that guy/gal with the boom box and Velcro-seamed police/nurse outfit spots you. And to think, they said they were leaving you in order to enter a monastery/convent!

The Fear of Flying Excuse

You'd love to invest in a tropical-weight tux/floral backless bridesmaid dress and fly seven hours to tropical Mamagualulu, but every time you even think about getting on a plane you break out in a sweat and have to run off to the nearest bathroom.

Introduction:
The Art of Extrication or How to Say "Gotta Go Now"

You didn't act quickly enough, or avoidance just didn't work. Now you're trapped in the social equivalent of handcuffs and a straitjacket —plus you're upside-down underwater!

Time to swing into action! Sure, the odds seem stacked against you, whether escaping from a romantic relationship without a painfully straightforward conversation or sending an awkward one-night stand packing before breakfast. And it can appear downright impossible to extricate yourself from comforting an endlessly teary friend, from the dreary monotony of everyday life, or from your own funeral.

This is when you must call upon The Escape Artist Within, that little voice deep down inside, the one that says over and over:

> *"I'm a devious worm and I can wriggle my way out of anything!"*

(It's best to keep that little voice to yourself on the street or crowded public transportation . . .)

In this section, you'll learn to free yourself from the locked trunk of a romantic relationship with just faux online infidelity and the wrong nicknames. You'll have that one-night stand flying out your door merely by quoting Hitchcock. And you'll liberate yourself from louts, lamenters, and last rites with nothing more than nudity, an onion, and some chilly liquid nitrogen.

Some escapes require minor preparation—the Santa Switcheroo for bolting from the office holiday parties, or the baby-in-the-bath self-rescue from door-to-door solicitors—but mostly they call for steely determination and relaxed-fit morals, a mindset that insists—Got to Go Now!

PLAN B:

The Art of Extrication or How to Say "Gotta Go Now"

A BLIND DATE

MUTUAL FRIENDS CLAIMED TO KNOW YOUR PERFECT match. Now you find yourself at the agreed-on café when in walks a sort of Frankenstein's Monster (see also: Bride of) of social rejects; someone combining bad breath, a Star Trek haircut, and orange knitwear in one utterly unappealing package. Fear not, though you walk in the valley of stinky dates, we have your escape routes mapped out:

The Mistaken Identity Escape

The mistaken identity ruse requires quick thinking and an expressionless poker face. Stash any identifying features. (You said you'd be wearing a blue scarf? Reading *The Economist*? Quick, bury them in a bag.) Avoid eye contact and when approached, reply with a regretful, "No, afraid not . . ." Check your watch and look around before leaving, as though you've been stood up.

The Friend's Phone Call Escape

Prearrange for a friend to call you 15 minutes into your date. They say: "So? What do you think?" You say: "Oh my God, when?! No, stay where you are, I'll be right there!" Excuse yourself by explaining that you're so sorry, of all times, but there's been a family crisis and/or your best friend is giving birth.

DOWNSIDE RISK: The loser you just met answers their phone first and says, "Oh my God, when?!"

The Master of Disguise Escape

Plan ahead and take a disguise along with you—a wig, a hat, a change of clothes, whatever you need to make sure you'd be unidentifiable. Identify your nearest bathroom on arrival. Then excuse yourself and slip into your new outfit.

You now should have no problems slipping past your would-be date and making good your escape.

The Classic Bathroom Escape

Arrive early to scout escape routes. Does the café bathroom have a window large enough to climb out? Will you need to fashion an escape ladder from napkins and tablecloths? Can you dart through the kitchen—"Health inspector!"—and out an alleyway?

NOTE: Always have at least two means of evacuation mapped out in case there's a problem with one of them.

The You Betrayed Me With Hello Escape

Announce after five minutes of small talk that you're feeling a special bond, a soulmate thing. Do they feel it, too? Ignore their answer. You've only felt this way about one other person, but they cheated on you. Use the bathroom. If they're still there when you return, ask who they've chatted up in your absence. Ask if they'd like to keep their options open, blind date other people. If they aren't leaving by then, storm out muttering, "Et tu, Brutus?"

The Contagious Disease Escape

You've just come from a medical appointment and it turns out you've got a touch—just a touch—of leprosy. The doctor says a two-year course of pills will clear it right up . . . Scratch your wrists violently, then tentatively reach out for his/her hand.

ESCAPES FOR HIM

The Hyper-Sensitive Escape

Confide anecdotes about being "too soft" in the eyes of your career-military dad. If they raise their hand to signal for the check, cringe like you're about to be struck.

The Pi-Throwing Escape

Say you really like pi. If she checks the menu, roll your eyes. You mean the number 3.14 etc. The ratio of a circle's circumference to its diameter? You can recite it to 500 decimal places!

The Mr. Sleaze Escape

Insist (despite your actual physical appearance) that exes called you "The Sledgehammer." Wink. Repeatedly mention your waterbed. Ask if she's ever done it in a dental office waiting area.

The Videogaming Escape

Which is her favorite? You're into Evil Farmer, where you get to kill off the city slickers building condos on your land with a super-laser pitchfork.

ESCAPES FOR HER

The Far Too Fragile Escape

Does he like little glass animals? You do so very much! You have a whole menagerie. You realize he hasn't seen them yet, but which one does he expect to like best?

The Tom-Beast Escape

You've always wanted a real man, but your last few boyfriends were wet noodles. Ask how long he'd last on a mechanical bull. Suggest arm-wrestling to see who gets the check. If any of this seems to be appealing to him, segue to talk of glass animals.

The Pride, Prejudice, and Pets Escape

Explain within minutes of meeting that you must hurry home to feed your seven cats—Elizabeth, Mr. Bingley, Mr. Darcy, Mr. Wickham, Colonel Fitzwilliam, Lady Catherine de Bourgh, and "Kitty" Bennet. If he tries to normalize this—saying you must really love Jane Austen to name all your cats after characters in *Pride and Prejudice*—act taken aback. Insist you don't know any Janes and you can name your own damn cats just fine.

YOUR JOB

WHEN LEAVING AN AWFUL JOB, GIVING SEVERAL WEEKS notice only means suffering through a dismal break-room goodbye party and an exit interview where you say it was all great but you just need to spend more time with your couch. Plus, if you quit you won't get the severance and unemployment benefits needed for a nice vacation. Here's how to take extra-early retirement:

The Resumé Escape

Strategically leave a copy of your resumé in one or two of the office photocopiers, especially the one that's near the busybody receptionist.

The Fake Lottery Win Escape

Pretend you've won the mega-jackpot but intend to keep working. During meetings doodle long strings of zeros in your checkbook; hold loud phone conversations in which you discuss Swiss bank accounts and interest accrual. Eventually, for the sake of office morale, you'll be asked to leave.

The Self-Outsourcing Escape

Prepare a detailed report on how they could send your job overseas for a fraction of what they pay you. Then, ask to combine your performance review where you get a raise for sharp thinking with your exit interview to, again, maximize company savings.

Magical Phrases to Make Your Job Disappear

They're not abracadabra but, used routinely, these should convince your employer to set you free:

> "... whenever I feel like it ..."

> "... not if I make my presentation first you won't ..."

> "... refuse to compromise my commitment to napping ..."

> "... We can easily meet that deadline by curving space-time ..."

> "... You said, 'youth in Asia,' and I heard 'euthanasia' so ..."

> "... our warranty is meant to set a mood more than anything ..."

> "... go ahead and call my supervisor; it's just me using a different voice ..."

> "... if our advertised guarantee spoke for itself, it would have a larynx ..."

> "... well maybe I find it inconvenient ..."

WORK ASSIGNMENTS

MAYBE YOU'RE A DENTAL HYGIENIST ASSIGNED A PATIENT who hasn't flossed in decades. Perhaps you're waiting tables when a notoriously obnoxious-yet-poor-tipping party of seventeen strolls in. Or you work in a shoe store and a guy with big stinky feet wants help trying on sandals. Don't quit (yet)! Here's how to play hopscotch on the job assignment minefield:

→ Flatter a more experienced colleague by asking how they'd approach the situation. Maintain your befuddlement and ask for a demonstration. As they perform your entire bummer task for you, express deep admiration for their far superior skills.

→ Mythical hero Hercules had to grab golden apples guarded by a hundred-headed dragon. He convinced Atlas, who had a brutal gig holding up the Earth and the Sky, to go instead as a change of pace. The lesson? Allow the waterlogged dishwasher to wait on that annoying dining party.

→ To magically elude grim chores, bypass smoke, given most office's restrictions, and go straight to mirrors. One should do the job if it's big enough and aimed at a vacant desk. You can then sit safely out of sight behind it.

THE OFFICE HOLIDAY PARTY

HOLIDAY PUNCH+CO-WORKERS=DANGER ZONE. HOLIDAY parties bring out a side of your co-workers you'd just rather not know about. So to avoid situations you'll have to pretend didn't happen the next business day, here's how to skip out on the one party you can't skip entirely:

The Significant Other's Holiday Party Escape

Your boyfriend/girlfriend's company picked the same evening for their party. (A friend can play the role in exchange for all they can eat and drink in 20 minutes.) Complain that you must "put in an appearance" at that stuffy affair across town.

The Customer Crisis Escape

It's well after normal working hours, perhaps Saturday night, but top management will admire your business-first! attitude leading to an early exit with regrets. This works best in fields like computer tech and plumbing. Not so well in, say, pet grooming and dry cleaning. But "emergency" poodle trims and stain removal requests might still be plausible.

The Santa Switcheroo Escape

Volunteer to play Santa. You're seen as a team player, putting up with employees' kids tugging your beard and poking your belly. After a photo taken in full regalia with your bosses, switch places with a Rent-a-Santa you've hired and enjoy your evening.

The Reverse Trojan Horse Escape

Cover your early exit from a holiday party at the office by noting that you have one last late shipment for an important client. Stowing yourself away in a large, well-ventilated container, call your pal with that Halloween UPS costume to come pick you up.

NOTE: Label container with your home address in case, by fluke, a real UPS guy shows up.

The Religious Restrictions Escape

Try saying the following:

> *"My deepest apologies for leaving early, but in my religion [name of obscure antibiotic with '-ism' added to end] there is also a winter solstice holiday and there are multiple gods at whose altars I must light candles, leave gift certificates, and generally genuflect before. In fact, there's a line-up of twenty-seven of them, so I'd better get a move on."*

PUBLIC DISPLAYS OF AFFECTION

YOUR NEW SQUEEZE CAN'T KEEP THEIR HANDS OFF YOU in public. It was sweet at first, but it's beginning to wear on you: the awkward snuggling into the same revolving door compartment, their palm on your butt while visiting grandpa, the big smooches outside work as your bosses troop by.

The Spatula Escape

Think of light poles and bus shelters not as urban streetscape, but as spatulas for gently prying away your clingy love muffin. Avoid an obvious beeline, but casually direct your conjoined promenade until a parking meter, street sign, or stationary panhandler forces you to part with such sweet sorrow. You'll then be free to continue on your way, unhampered by your loved one's affections. Putting your hands in your pockets will help to avoid the situation happening again.

The Good Samaritan Escape

Insist on aiding the blind, the elderly, children, and semi-lame dogs crossing streets and boarding buses. Your flame will understand that you need both hands free, although they may think it odd when you dash back and forth, juggling all four deeds at once.

The Honesty Escape

Sit down (in private), take both their hands in yours, and concede that perhaps you're too self-conscious at times. But you're just not sure that your nephew's kindergarten graduation was the right time and place for them to be teething on your earlobe. Prepare to sleep on the couch for a night or two . . .

The Private Displays of Affection Escape

Exhaust your beloved in private. Like a boxer who throws all their best punches in the early rounds, they'll stagger outside weak from their exertions, all nuzzled, kissed, and groped out. Wear high collars to cover the hickey that looks like you had heart surgery through your neck.

The Competitive PDAs Escape

Consider the mating praying mantis: At first, the male can't get enough of the female. Then she bites his head off—which presumably mellows him out. So, give back double the PDAs you're getting. Are they pinching your butt? Pinch theirs with both hands. Check-out line kisses? Try face licking.

A TEARY FRIEND

WE ALL HAVE ONE FRIEND WHO LIVES AMID PERPETUAL melodrama: lovers always leaving, pets passing weekly, and forever getting canned. Sure, they were cheating, their cats are ancient, and the jobs are temp gigs, but the forecast is still for streaking mascara and deep drifts of wet tissues. How can you give a nod toward comforting companionship yet get on with your day?

The Giving Them Their Space Excuse

The key to a graceful departure for less gloomy climes is to offer them The Gift of Solitude. After all, they can't properly grieve their lost loser (". . . lover, of course, did I say loser?"), pet, or job with you hovering about offering your wan reassurances.

The Onion of Neurotic Empathy Escape

To cut things short, demonstrate an empathy so intense that they wind up comforting you. Bring an onion and pocketknife, sneak off for some surreptitious slicing, then return teary and red-eyed. Explain that you're just so upset about their situation you can't bear it. One last big hug and they'll send you off with solace and tissues.

The Buying More Tissues Escape

If your teary friend manages to use up all of their tissues, they'll inadvertently offer you an unmissable escape opportunity. No bother at all. You'll just dash to the store and be right back. Failing to return, you can always explain later that you ran into that lame ex of theirs (and lit into them good), ran into their ex-boss (ditto), and/or ran over someone else's cat.

The Other Stop On Your Saintly Rounds Escape

You must aid someone else suffering in a similar situation. And this other person is not holding it together anywhere near as well. It sounds like a complete gibbering breakdown. This fortifies your teary friend's ego as you head for fun.

UNIVERSAL ESCAPE #3:

The Driving Someone to E.R. Escape

This ace-up-the-sleeve is normally as obvious as a Blind Date Phone Call Escape, but your friend's probably too weepy to notice. Some E.R.-worthy ideas:

KITCHEN BLENDER ACCIDENT: "I must hurry—at least they've got the fingertips on ice!"

MEDICATION REACTION: "I must hurry—his erection has lasted more than four hours!"

TECHNO-MELTDOWN: "I must hurry—the DVD player remote 'fast-forwarded' their pacemaker!"

UNWANTED ADVANCES

THE MURPHY'S LAW OF BEING HIT ON? IT'S ALWAYS BY the wrong people. At work, a "stress relief" neck massage comes via the office computer geek. And the hand on your hip at the bar comes from a staggering mess who spills their fruity drink on you. Here are ways to call off the mangy dogs:

The There Must Be Some Mistake Escape

Delivered with a smile, these lines make it clear that you're not interested. At work: "Are you trying to type an e-mail? Because that's my neck you've been fingering." At the bar: "Good thing I'm too drunk to notice you just hit on me and get all freaked out."

The You Have Got To Be Kidding Escape (Nastier)

When it is time to lay down the law . . . At work: "Maybe in an alternative universe that move's seductive, not just creepy." The bar: "There's truly nothing hotter than someone an hour or two from the dry heaves."

The Clandestine Bathroom Meeting Escape

This classic escape is a form of misdirection. Pretend you're hot for him, and ask him to hook up in the women's washroom. Tell him to wait for you in the farthest stall. Then quickly exit the building, pausing only to inform security there's a creepy guy hiding in the lavatory.

ESCAPES FOR HIM

The Perfume Allergy Escape

As she leans in seductively, wrinkle up your face and blink rapidly as if you're tearing up. Explain that you suffer from extreme fragrance sensitivity to perfumes. Clutch your throat and make a wheezing escape.

The Communicable Rash Escape

Grab their wandering hand and ask if they've ever had a rash from poison oak. Go off about the terrible itching you're suffering. Invite them to join you in a bath of soothing oatmeal as you scratch at your abdomen with both hands.

The Shocking Family Secret Escape

If the advancee is someone you've known a while, you can let them down easily by explaining that before your great-aunt Floosianna passed away (they might remember, you had to skip their dinner party to visit her in the hospital) she called you to her bedside and let you in on some family history. She'd had a child by another man, and that child's son/daughter is . . . well, they can work it out. Yes, you explain, we're actually second cousins. So, please, this is just too weird . . .

ESCAPES FOR HER

The Stalking Brutal Ex Escape

Tell friends, acquaintances, and co-workers about a jealous ex with an ugly police record and/or an overprotective sibling whom you rarely see since they joined an elite counterterrorist squad. If the guy hitting on you doesn't believe that you have a pathological ex who wears brass knuckles monogrammed with your initials, or a sister who knows nine ways to kill a man with his tropical drink umbrella, tell them to ask anyone you know—or find out for themselves.

The Static Electricity Escape

Scuff your feet on carpets until you've built up a charge that stands your hair on end and gives anyone coming too close a nearly heart-stopping shock. Repeat as necessary.

The Fragility Escape

"Thanks for the offer, but my herniated cervical disc means your clumsy groping neck massage could leave me paralyzed from the chin down" or "If you don't mind—I'm mortally ticklish—which tends to set off my asthma!"

A DOG'S UNWANTED ADVANCES

WHEN IT COMES TO DOGS, "I THINK HE LIKES YOU!" CAN be five very awkward words. And if he gets any friendlier one of your legs is going to have puppies. This is not the time to roll over. If its owner won't intervene, here's how to bring that puppy to heel:

The Squirt in the Snout Escape

Wait until the furry angel's owner turns their back or leaves the room, then a fire off a quick squirt of water at their snout to back them off. Wetting your fingers and flinging the droplets might also work in a pinch. You could also try positive reinforcement by getting him to sit and stay, then feeding him whatever you can get your hands on.

The Scarecrow Leg Escape

Think of this as putting a chain-smoker on the nicotine patch. If you've faced this hairy humper before, then come prepared with a second pair of pants or pantyhose. When the dog goes into romantic mode, quickly stuff the spare clothing with throw pillows, blanket, etc. and, like a toreador distracting a charging bull, offer a non-you alternative.

BEING DUMPED

THE RELATIONSHIP IS WINDING DOWN, BUT YOU'RE JUST not ready to be dumped right now, not until you have a Plan B in place and can do the dumping yourself. For such tricky situations we suggest:

The Abbreviated Voice Mail Escape

Some boyfriends/girlfriends may try leaving their "it's not you, it's me" speech on your voice mail. Not if you reprogram it to only accept, say, a 20-second message they won't!

The Loud Nightclub Escape

Meet your nearly-ex only in places with electric bands or 110-decibel sound systems. Nothing inhibits a break-up spiel like having to yell it in public. If they try, smile and shrug to indicate you can't hear a word. Afterward? Your ears are still ringing!

The Invented Crises Escape

Your car was towed, your waterbed leaked, and/or you had a bit of gas during a big job interview. Only the heartless would dump you now. If they still try, pre-emptively misinterpret their arrival: "You don't have to say anything, just being here is so supportive."

THE PARTY BORE

LIKE A BARNACLE ON A YACHT HULL, THE DULLEST person at the party has latched onto you. They're talking non-stop about computer upgrades, their mom's hip surgery, or their new hobby, building miniature replicas of nuclear power plants. You finally understand the phrase, "Bored to tears." Time to act!

The Swift Palm-Off Escape

Snag a passerby and say, "Hi Chris! [insert dullard's name] here is telling me all about post-surgical sponge baths. Didn't you have to do that?" "Valerie! Didn't you just upgrade your PC? How crazy was that?" Eventually, someone will mistakenly venture an opinion—now they are trapped in the bore's web of tedium and you can use the brief distraction to dart away.

The Strength in Numbers Escape

Same as above, but to end the cycle of victimization gather as many innocent bystanders into the orbit of you and this lightless sun as you can. Eventually, the volume and variety of chatter will, by natural evolution, steer the group's conversation away from computer code customization and back to who's sleeping with whom, bizarre celebrity news, and the last party where you all got really drunk together. The Bore will eventually drift off, in search of new victims.

The Party Host Forced To Mingle Escape

Say, "Sounds like building scale-model nuke plants is downright addictive! But listen to me! I could talk about this all night but I've got to make sure the rest of these potted plants are properly watered." This may seem odd if the party isn't yours, but hurry off before that issue gets raised.

If you happen to bump into the Party Bore at some point in the evening, use this tried and tested technique to get rid of them again:

The Looking For The Toilet Excuse

Look pleased to see them, clap them on the shoulder, and ask them immediately if they know where the toilet is. If they do know, tell them they're a godsend, and elegantly turn your clap on the shoulder into a lever as you sweep past them and head for the door. If the party is at your house, this excuse may look a little thin. In this case, ask them where so-and-so (such as your wife) is. Rush off swiftly on a task of great importance, leaving them confused and bewildered.

The Diversion Escape

Point out someone across the room—anyone they don't know—and suggest they'd be the perfect person with whom to discuss scale-model power plants. Apparently, they built a natural gas refinery out of pipe cleaners and Popsicle sticks and it won some sort of prize for its detail. Say that you'll rejoin their conversation in just a moment, then make your heart-pounding dash back to freedom.

If you run into the tiresome talker later, admit you stand corrected: "You're right, they didn't build that model, but I think I know who did. Let me just go look for them."

The Basic Instinct Escape

Apologetically interrupt and ask if they believe in love at first sight. Point at someone across the room and whisper, "Wish me luck!" Hurry over to the stranger and/or old friend you'd never date and ask, "Do you think it's possible to be bored to death?"

A DISMAL PARTY

THE DRINKS ARE WATERY, THE DIP RUNNY, AND THE music too loud yet impossible to dance to. Among the few people who showed up there's not a soul you'd consider flirting with. Sure, your escape may be harder if you're the host, but do yourself a party favor anyway:

The Beer Run Escape

You're just going to the corner store and will be right back. Of course, you won't return. If you're ever asked, have a surreal excuse-story ready: You ran into Jane Goodall! Not the world-famous chimpanzee expert, your childhood sweetheart, that Jane Goodall. (Women may opt for Tim Berners-Lee, "not the guy who invented World Wide Web . . .")

The Sudden Seduction Escape

If you're a woman, approach any single guy by himself and run your finger along his neck while whispering "Let's get out of here." A long shot? Scientific research shows it works 97.4 percent of the time. Dangerous? Quite possibly. Once the guy has escorted you to your car, it is time to make your excuses. See: A Blind Date, page 38, for your next step.

The Psychedelic Freak-Out Escape

Confide to your host that before the party you had a salad and tossed in mushrooms that your odd "amateur shaman" roommate left in the refrigerator. Right now everyone at the party looks like glowing purple gargoyles. Apologies, but you've got to go home and lie down in a dark quite room for about 17 hours until the psilocybin wears off.

IF IT'S YOUR OWN PARTY...

The Relocation to a Bar Escape

Sadly announce that neighbors have complained about the noise. Suggest that the whole group adjourn to a nearby pub. And the first round's on you! Once at the bar, pay the tab and find a better party.

The Camera Phone Scavenger Hunt Escape

Provide a list of stuff they'll need to snap and e-mail you. The first four things are in your home. The next three just outside. The next two inside a cab or bus. The last one is way across town. After submitting all ten you'll text them where to find their prize. Having sent your guests away, be decent and hide some champagne at the hunt's end.

The Faux Surprise Escape

For when you just don't care. Buzzing someone in from downstairs, announce that it's actually their birthday. After everyone hides, douse the lights and crack the door. Once the big "Surprise!" is launched upon the confused latecomer, all will look for you to explain, but under cover of darkness and commotion you've snuck out the back.

THE SCENE OF A ONE-NIGHT STAND

IT WAS MAJOR BEER GOGGLES OR LUST AT FIRST SIGHT that's left you queasy with second thoughts. The point is: You've got to leave fast (or get this ludicrous lover out of your house) with assurances that it was really great and/or nothing to be ashamed of. You'll call them—and this time by their correct name!—really soon. Here's how to get out of there quick-smart:

→ Sorry to skip breakfast, but your Sex Addicts Anonymous meeting starts in ten minutes. As for lunch, your Genital Warts and Herpes Support Group is having a picnic to celebrate 30 days without a major visible outbreak. But you'll definitely stay in touch!

→ Discreetly set your watch forward eight hours, then bolt from bed, hastily grabbing your clothes and pointing out the time in Beijing/Dubai/The Hague. It's dawn here but late afternoon over there and you've got a major dollar deal to close!

→ You've got a full-grown Great Dane. If you don't hurry home to take him out for his morning ritual, your place won't be habitable for months.

→ You've already lied about your job's glamour to get them in the sack— meat-slicing at a deli counter became "veterinary surgeon"—so now that there's an emergency they'll understand that you must run to the aid of an injured thoroughbred. Next time, however, a V.I.P. breakfast is definitely on you!

→ Wake them at daybreak and ask if they've ever heard of the Code Delta Force. Your real name isn't Michael/Kate, but that's not important now. You must leave right away. No time for breakfast, and they certainly can't tag along where you're going.

IF THEY'RE AT YOUR PLACE

→ Don a collar or habit left over from Halloween, say you'll treasure the memory but your vows rule out repeats. If it's Saturday, pin a fabric coaster in your hair and explain you've got to run—you're presiding over the Greenblatt bar mitzvah in an hour.

→ Slip into another room—a closet will do—and fake an early morning argument with someone unseen. Return to bed and explain that your mom lives with you and "She just goes a little mad sometimes." If they aren't

A) sufficiently creeped out; or

B) recognizing that you're quoting Hitchcock, lay it on thicker: "Oh, but she's as harmless as one of those stuffed birds, etc." Continue until they turn down your shower offer and hurry away.

→ That was terrific, but another "client" is arriving at 9 a.m. so you've got to get cleaned up. Wink and add: "Last night was so good, let's say it's on the house."

AN ORGY

A FRIEND OF A FRIEND INVITES YOU TO "AN INTIMATE gathering" but it turns out that wearing pants makes you overdressed for the occasion. You consider yourself sexually liberated, but this is not your thing. Besides, the assembled group looks like an X-rated version of the bar scene in *Star Wars*. How do you suavely skip out on a ménage à douzaine?

→ Insist that everyone at the orgy has to play Six Degrees of My Sleazy Ex-Brother-In-Law Ray. (This should buy you time to escape through a bathroom window.)

→ You have this major hang-up—you can only have group sex with a prime number of people.

→ You've always considered a hot tub packed with naked people to be "human soup"—and you're vegetarian.

→ You kind of like to be wined and dined first—which means, 7, 8, 9 . . . twelve dinners!

→ You just wouldn't feel right cheating on your Tuesday night sex group.

UNWANTED HOUSEGUESTS

YOU'VE HAD WEEKEND VISITORS—FRIENDS WITH OUT- of-control kids, old pals who were too loud too late, and/or persnickety relatives who disparaged your housekeeping. You thought the worst was over, but now they're talking about staying a few more days. How do you get them out of here?

The Not-So-Subtle Hints Escape

Rise early to prepare a hearty "final morning" breakfast. Point out that it's a lovely day to travel. Set the table with lovingly stitched needlepoint placemats quoting Benjamin Franklin to the effect that fish and visitors both stink after three days.

The Major Fumigation Escape

Appear at breakfast with a packed suitcase. You didn't think they'd still be around, so exterminators are coming today to absolutely bomb the place. You're so glad that the bedbugs, roaches, and black widows didn't bother them during their stay.

The Criminal Forensics Escape

The police think some awful business may have occurred here before you moved in. They're coming today to dust for prints, spray something that reveals blood residues, and yank up floorboards to see if anything—or anyone—is secreted in the crawl spaces.

The Bed and Breakfast Escape

You hope they've enjoyed their stay, but you've rented out their room to tourists who arrive today. Of course, the plausibility may vary: Victorian cottage in historic district, easy; apartment next to highway ramp, hard.

The Resident Poltergeist Escape

While it requires the sort of poker face usually available to normal people only via extensive Botox injections, this may be the most satisfying of houseguest ejections. While they're out, you hurl their belongings around the spare bedroom and/or toss them out the window. You could also routinely awaken them in the wee small hours by randomly pounding on the floorboards with a broom handle and/or playing The Dark Side of the Moon with speakers pressed against their wall and the bass pushed up to "10." Explain that your home's haunted by an obnoxious spirit who seems to have little patience with longer-term guests.

The Other Guests Soon Arriving Escape

You have other guests arriving:

A) Friends coming into town for an annual snake and spider swap meet.

B) Your ex with their new lover. As you know better than anyone, they can get a bit "noisy" at night.

A ROMANTIC RELATIONSHIP

EVERYTHING YOU USED TO FIND DELIGHTFUL NOW makes you feel homicidal. You've decided your relationship needs to end. When you need to generate major loopholes in your implied romantic contract, here are your best moves:

The Sane, Mature, and Thoughtful Escape

Sit down face-to-face someplace where you won't get interrupted but can quickly exit. (For example, International Space Station, bad. Park bench, good.) Explain in a clear, firm voice that you've had a change of heart, it's not them it's you and that you wish them the best . . . (adding in muttering aside) with the next poor soul they afflict.

The Cell Phone Escape

Insist on answering cell calls whenever. No matter how intense the conversation, in the middle of sex, etc. Choose the humpback whale flatulence ringtone. Program the phone to ring frequently or hire a professional service to call constantly.

The Pathological Liar Escape

Cultivate a strong sense of mistrust. Example: At restaurants, take big bites of their food while they're using the bathroom, then insist—with their meal's residue prominently wedged in your gums—that you have no idea what they're talking about.

The Terrible Quest Escape

You're planning on a tattoo. A whole-body circus freak number: "It'll take all my savings and hurt like hell, but I'll carry an accurate, complete, topographical map of Middle Earth with me to my grave." A temporary henna sample, dabbed with fresh ketchup, should send them packing.

The Extreme Rubber Necking Escape

A roving eye is nothing to apologize about. Cultivate one and then turn it up a few notches . . . Give a long sideways glance and emit a low whistle every time an attractive person of their gender goes by. Insist you're just looking. Gradually reduce your discrimination threshold until you're ogling statues, lawn gnomes, and saucily crawling bugs.

The Sexual Peccadilloes Escape

Now that you're so comfortable together in bed you'd like to:

A) Pretend you're both kangaroos—wearing front-facing fanny packs stuffed with plush toys and hopping around the bedroom.

B) Pretend you're both praying mantises. Insist on being the one who suddenly bites the other's head off.

C) Pretend they're applying for a mortgage. Keep asking them about credit scores and income documentation as things progress.

ESCAPES FOR HIM

Never shave or remove any hair. From any body part. Ever.

Assure her that you think her breast size is fine—constantly.

Fill your medicine cabinet with half-emtpy herpes creams/pills and say, "They're leftovers from ex-girlfriends, never used 'em myself."

When you're sent out to buy tampons come back with a case of beer instead.

ESCAPES FOR HER

Never shave or remove any hair. From any body part. Ever.

Assure him you don't mind that he's balding—constantly.

Fill your medicine cabinet with half-empty containers of yeast infection creams/pills and insist that he shouldn't worry his "cute little rapidly balding head" about it.

When you're sent out to buy beer, just never come back.

UNWANTED
HOUSE-CALLERS

YOU BOUND TO THE FRONT DOOR EXPECTING A VITAL delivery. Instead, it's a politely insistent coterie of Jehovah's Witnesses spreading the good word. Or perhaps it's someone painfully earnest, selling cookware, cosmetics, or encyclopedias. Maybe you grab your ringing phone expecting a friend's callback, but no, it's a charity or political fund-raiser. You don't want to seem disrespectful, unkind, or ungenerous, you just want to become instantly invisible and unavailable. In the absence of a Harry Potter cloak, we've got your means of egress right here:

The Crazed and Dazed Escape

If you're a guy, quickly squeeze into a wife or girlfriend's cocktail dress (the bad fit is a plus) before answering the door. If you're a woman, apply raccoon mascara and lipstick that surrounds your mouth like the rings of Saturn and extends to one ear. Slapping at imaginary bugs on the door frame, staring fearfully at their feet, or squint as though you haven't seen the sun in days while asking "Who really sent you?!" This should quickly send even the most fervent solicitors back-pedaling, explaining that they have "the wrong address."

The Back Door & More Escape

A surreptitious and spy-like escape out the back door, coupled with a re-entry sequence will have callers confused for weeks: On hearing a knock at the door, glance out the window or peephole and assess the threat. Then quickly exit out your back way. Besides not answering your door, this escape lets you pre-empt return visits. Walk around front and address the people on your doorstep as if you're just Mr./Ms. Neighbor Passing By. Try "They work third shift at that big gun factory, so they are probably sleeping," or "You'll be waiting awhile. The person who lives there just got sent to prison."

The Tele-Ejection Phrase List

If you had Caller I.D. or glanced at it you'd never have picked up the phone. But it's not too late to make this call a quick one. Just cut out the following, have it laminated, and keep it right next the phone along with emergency and take-out pizza phone numbers. Be sure to alternate your lines so their delivery stays fresh:

". . . you've reached my cell phone. I can't talk while driving because I get dis—" (scream, abruptly hang up)

". . . you've caught me with the runs, let me just switch to the phone over by the toilet. . ."

". . . what a coincidence, you've reached another call center, I'm recording this to ensure quality service. . ."

". . . [smash a magazine down next to mouth piece] Sorry about that, bit of a cockroach problem. You were saying?. . ."

". . . I'd know that voice anywhere, did you go to [your high school]? . . . I know it's you, how'd you wind up doing this?. . ."

". . . this isn't one of those scary bits where it winds up you're calling me from inside my own home is it?"

DOING HOUSEWORK

YOU AGREED WITH YOUR SPOUSE, ROOMMATE, OR LIVE-IN to take turns doing the dishes, dusting, mopping, vacuuming, and bathroom scrubbing—but after a full day of work you feel a state of Zen detachment from such mundane worldly squalor. You can't skip your share entirely, but here's how to sweep a bunch under the rug:

→ Negotiate a peace treaty dividing your home into public zones for visitors that require serious cleaning and private areas, where chaos may reign. If you're not the cleaning type, the goal is to limit guests to the living room, dining area, and one bathroom.

→ It's true that the living room still has teetering stacks of old pizza boxes, CDs, DVDs, and magazines, but you removed all the unused icons on your shared "desktop" and then emptied the "recycling bin," so you're making progress.

→ It may not look like you cleaned up very much, but you've cleared a precise path among the Legos, dirty socks, and old magazines, generating a contemplative clockwise maze that aligns your home's flow of chi life force with both the fire sign (spicy snacks) and the water sign (the hot tub).

→ Dust, molds, and cleaning fluid fumes can give some folks fits. If you failed to make this excuse initially you'll need to get busy with fake wheezing.

→ After paying a professional housecleaner to come and do your share, confide that you have an old friend that your partner's never met who suffers from an overpowering need to clean. It's one of those conditions that usually responds well to medication, but there's an occasional setback—it's a chemical imbalance. He/she is coming for a visit tomorrow and if they should happen to show up in some sort of "maid" outfit and start wiping the place down, just act like it's the most normal thing in the world.

→ If you live alone, simply seal off the front door with that yellow police tape and, insisting you'd "rather not talk about it," invite visitors to dine out.

→ You were not "napping instead of cleaning," you:

A) slipped on a banana peel that fell out of the kitchen trash, bruised your coccyx, and passed out from the pain.

B) unclogged the sink with a plunger, which suddenly popped loose, hurtling you backward onto the recliner.

C) were trying to finally toss out that old souvenir boomerang, but it circled back and whacked you in the back of the head.

PLANT AND PET CARE,
HOUSE-SITTING, AND/OR BABYSITTING

YOU OWE A FAVOR BECAUSE SOMEONE HELPED YOU FIX A
flat tire in the rain, gave you a late-night ride home, or pretended
to be your possessive date (so you couldn't dance with Earl/Tina at
the office holiday party). But now they're asking you to take care
of their botanical garden, care for five cats, keep an eye on their
place, and/or baby-sit. Here's how to take a stand against sitting:

The Just Not This Time Excuse

You know you owe them, but a temporary conflict gives you another turn
at the Wheel of Favors. You'll pay off your moral debt at a cheaper rate if
you can delay until: a) you've both forgotten their original favor or b) they
ask you to pick up take-out.

The Phobias Excuse

"Involuntarily" shudder, then confide that you suffer from botanophobia
(fear of plants), felinophobia (fear of cats), copro-felinophobia (fear of cat
poop), and pedophobia (fear of children). For good measure you can
throw in felino-pedo-pediophobia (fear of kids' cat dolls). Reel this off while
wringing your hands and taking nervous shallow breaths.

The Allergies Excuse

Unfortunately, your biological responses won't allow you to help. Ask what kind of dog/cat/bird/plants they need cared for. Then explain with a sad shake of the head that you are violently allergic to [specific type of dog/cat/bird/plants they just named, slip in "non-related children" if necessary]. Learn to say the phrase "terrible hives and potentially life-threatening anaphylactic shock" so that it rolls off your tongue as easily as "I almost had to sit Ed/Edie's dog, let's go grab a beer."

THE NUCLEAR EXCUSE

The spoken-on-one-breath truth,
conveyed with one foot already out the door.

"Sorry, I've done some math and you can count me out. I don't think that fixing a flat (really you just held the lug bolts and umbrella) is anywhere near the equivalent of sifting reeking cat poo then opening cans of gag-inducing liver-in-sauce while I kick away your yowling pests rubbing up against me like perverts on a rush-hour bus. A few more taps on the moral calculator reveals that a ride home (you were going my direction anyway and hoping to get asked in for tea) does not equal three or four visits to your musty flat in support of your Little Shop of Horrors rainforest plant fetish or checking to see that some diabolical burglar isn't on eBay giddily auctioning off your collection of airport gift-shop world capitals snow globes or margin-scribbled Harry Potter hardcovers. As for pretending to be my jealous mate at the office party, not even that plus the promise of a future kidney donation is worth an evening stuck in the broken-toy-strewn eighth circle with your sticky-fingered snot-nosed impulse-disordered hyperactive demon child."

THE DREARY MONOTONY
OF EVERYDAY LIFE

SO YOUR DAY GOES SOMETHING LIKE THIS: MORNING bathroom routine. Eat mega-fiber cereal. Wait in traffic, wait for download, replace printer toner, ride elevator with someone humming off-key. Sit in meetings. Grab lunch at franchise with a million identical set-ups. Call "busy" friend; avoid a bore by saying you're busy. Read "zany" email sent to you at work. Pick up dry cleaning. Jog on treadmill. Eat cereal for dinner. Web surf. Channel flip. Stop! Here are exit options from zombiehood:

The Snow Globe Escape

Shake up everything. Commute by skateboard. Wear your watch on the "wrong" wrist. Go to zoos on lunch hour and get licked by exotic species. Make meeting comments in iambic pentameter. Volunteer at a birthing class—and a hospice. Study ancient martial arts—and harmonica. Grow some of your own food. Or just triple your coffee intake.

The Time Shuffle Escape

Have dinner for breakfast. If possible, work different hours or days. Work until 1 a.m. Saturday, spend Tuesday afternoon in a dive bar. Go bat-watching and do solar astronomy. Eat different color foods based on the day of the week. Use a traditional Bangladesh calendar: Celebrate New Year's on the first of Boishakh, Pôhela Boishakh (April 14).

The Make Yourself Famous Escape

Hire a stylist. And a web designer. Create the ultimate social-media profile. Add a self-promoting blog. Make "appearances." Hire a publicist. Set up a red carpet to the front door of your studio apartment. Hire a paparazzo or two to follow you—to get the ball rolling. Develop press leaks. Deny romantic links with other celebrities. Randomly lunge at a paparazzo. Use your web page to "set the record straight" about your wee-hours hot-tubbing with theoretical physicist Stephen Hawking, and daily snorting of crushed Ritalin pills followed by marathon poolside spelling bees with your thesaurus-toting entourage. And so on.

The Mix It Up Escape

Start a weird benign rumor and do everything you legally can to spread it. Examples: Swiss cheese holes spell stencilled messages in Braille. Dalmatians have been cross-bred with zebras to create huge dogs bearing hairy exclamation points. You can set off airport metal detectors by thinking about pots and pans. Mention it to gossips. Post it on bulletin boards. Start a blog about it. Chart the Google citations and the major media echoes.

The Your Life Is a Movie Escape

Why not "You: The Movie"? With iPods holding thousands of songs, you've got an instant soundtrack. Add narrow glasses to put everyday life in DVD widescreen "letterbox" format. Mull camera angles. Finish meetings and meals by shouting, "That's a wrap!"

YOUR OWN FUNERAL

AN OPEN CASKET COULD ADD INSULT TO YOUR BIGGEST injury ever: "Whoa, is he wearing rouge and lipstick?" "Actually, she looks good, considering . . . " And if you're into reincarnation, there's a certain been-there-done-that aspect. Here's how to go from "dearly departed" to "later, dude."

The Suspended Animation Escape

Insist on cryopreserving your body at temperatures as low as minus -320°F. The thinking is that centuries from now science will advance enough to revive you. The sheer indignity of your survivors gathering around a steel tank of liquid nitrogen holding your remains like a freezer-section fishstick should can any memorial service. When they find out you've put all of their inheritance towards paying for the chilling tab, your ceremony will be put on hold until you revive and croak again.

The Outlive Everyone Escape

Outlive everybody—granted, a bit tricky given the role of genes and the environment. However, you can do your bit. Don't smoke. Pursue weight-bearing and cardiovascular workouts, eat low-fat, high-fiber, omega-3-laden meals, practice stress reduction and safe regular sex in a mutually supportive emotionally committed relationship. Sure, some rotten thing will get you anyway, but by then, everyone you knew will be long gone, so you can skip having a funeral.

The Pre-Emptive Strike Escape

Hold your funeral while you're still alive. Eulogize the "old you"—that smoking overweight disorganized procrastinator. Cremate your last smokes. Bury your "relaxed fit" shower curtain and never-opened "Habits of Organized Persons" calendar. Also declare dead your dreams of movie stardom, sports fame, and/or becoming a celebrity chef. Then hold a great big party. By the time your real funeral rolls around, it'll be too redundant to bother.

The Insufferable Living Will Escape

Compose a legal document (i.e. living will) specifying you wish to be kept alive by any means necessary: No matter how many machines are involved, even if you're no more sentient than a zucchini, have zero chance of recovery and damn the cost. By the time a janitor tripping over an electrical cord puts the kibosh on your veggie preserves, friends and family—disgusted by your egocentrism—will kill off your funeral.

The Fake Your Own Death Escape

Fake your own death. Overlook the creepiness, blatant illegality, and the conspiracy theories that may eventually follow. Think of it as giving friends and family—informed beforehand, so they're not upset—a golden escape option. Yes, everyone you know can get out of bad blind dates, pathetic parties, boring business meetings, hellish housework, lame dancing, horrid houseguests, and one-night stands gone awry. Officially speaking, they've got a funeral to go to!

Index

METRO BOOKS
New York

An Imprint of Sterling Publishing
1166 Avenue of the Americas
New York, NY 10036

Conceived and produced by

Elwin Street Productions

3 Percy Street

London W1T 1DE

United Kingdom

www.elwinstreet.com

ISBN 978-1-4351-5795-8

For information about custom editions, special sales, and premium and corporate purchases,

please contact Sterling Special Sales at 800-805-5489 or specialsales@sterlingpublishing.com.

Illustrations: iStock/leremy

Manufactured in China

2 4 6 8 10 9 7 5 3 1

www.sterlingpublishing.com